LOS CAMIONES DE VOLTEO
DUMP TRUCKS

Dan Osier

Traducción al español: Eida de la Vega

PowerKiDS press.

New York

Published in 2014 by The Rosen Publishing Group, Inc.
29 East 21st Street, New York, NY 10010

First Edition

Editor: Amelie von Zumbusch
Book Design: Andrew Povolny
Photo Research: Katie Stryker

Traducción al español: Eida de la Vega

Photo Credits: Cover Ivaschenko Roman/Shutterstock.com; p. 5 Andrey N Ecrrov/Shutterstock.com; p. 7 Viktor1/Shutterstock.com; p. 9 Orange Line Media/Shutterstock.com; p. 11 Goran Bogicevic/Shutterstock.com; p. 13 Bram van Broekhoven; p. 15 GTS Production/Shutterstock.com; p. 17 Wollertz/Shutterstock.com; p. 19 ndoeljindoel/Shutterstock.com; p. 21 Dragunov/Shutterstock.com; p. 23 Zacarias Pereira da Mata/Shutterstock.com.

Library of Congress Cataloging-in-Publication Data

Osier, Dan, author.
Dump trucks = Los camiones de volteo / by Dan Osier ; translated by Eida de la Vega. — First edition.
     pages cm. — (Construction site = En construcción)
English and Spanish.
Includes index.
ISBN 978-1-4777-3292-2 (library)
1. Dump trucks—Juvenile literature. 2. Construction equipment—Juvenile literature. I. Vega, Eida de la, translator. II. Osier, Dan. Dump trucks. III. Osier, Dan. Dump trucks. Spanish. IV. Title. V. Title: Camiones de volteo.
TL230.15.O8518 2014
629.225—dc23

2013022465

Websites: Due to the changing nature of Internet links, PowerKids Press has developed an online list of websites related to the subject of this book. This site is updated regularly. Please use this link to access the list:
www.powerkidslinks.com/cs/dump/
Manufactured in the United States of America

CPSIA Compliance Information: Batch #W14PK3 For Further Information contact Rosen Publishing, New York, New York at 1-800-237-9932

Contenido

Los camiones de volteo 4

Alrededor del mundo 12

Los camiones de volteo en acción 16

Palabras que debes saber 24

Índice 24

Contents

Dump Trucks 4

Around the World 12

Dump Trucks at Work 16

Words to Know 24

Index 24

Los **camiones de volteo** llevan **cargas** grandes.
Luego las descargan.

Dump trucks carry big **loads**.
Then they dump them out.

5

La carga va en la cama
del camión.

The load goes in the truck bed.

Una lona puede cubrir la cama.
Evita que la carga se derrame.

A tarp may cover the bed. It keeps the load from spilling out.

La carga debe equilibrarse bien. Si no lo está, el camión se puede volcar.

The load must be balanced right. If it is not, the truck could tip over.

A los camiones de volteo también se les llama volquetes.

Dump trucks are called tipper lorries in Great Britain.

12

13

Los camiones de obras son los más grandes. ¡No pueden circular por las carreteras!

Off-highway dump trucks are the biggest kind. They are too big to go on roads!

Para manejar un camión de volteo hay que tener una licencia para conducir vehículos comerciales.

You need a commercial driver's license to drive a dump truck.

Los **trabajadores de la construcción** usan camiones de volteo.

Construction workers use dump trucks.

18

Los mineros y los granjeros también los usan.

People in mines use them, too. So do people on farms.

¿Alguna vez has visto un camión de volteo?

Have you ever seen a dump truck?

22

23

PALABRAS QUE DEBES SABER / WORDS TO KNOW

(el) trabajador de la construcción

construction worker

(el) camión de volteo

dump truck

(la) carga

load

ÍNDICE

C
cama, 8, 10
carga(s), 4, 6, 8, 10

L
lona, 8

V
volquetes, 12

INDEX

B
bed, 6, 8

L
load(s), 4, 6, 8, 10

T
tarp, 8
tipper lorries, 12